SONGS FROM TH[

JEREMY SANDFORD

SONGS FROM THE ROADSIDE

sung by Romani Gypsies in the West Midlands

with drawings

by

PETER UPTON

THE REDLAKE PRESS
Clun
1995

© text Jeremy Sandford 1995
The Redlake Press
   Brook House, Clun, Shropshire
ISBN 1 870019 11 3
Printed in Great Britain

Published with the financial support of West Midlands Arts

For

The Romani Nation

ACKNOWLEDGEMENTS

I have received extremely generous help from our Gypsy community. In particular I'd like to thank Harry and Evelyn Smith, George Smith, Amos Smith, Wisdom 'Wiggy' Smith, the late Eliza Smith, Bill Kerswell, Danny Brazil, Johnny 'Pops' Connors, Mary Delaney, Mark O'Gallaidhe, Tom Odley, Ted Atkinson, Mik and Susie Darling, Duncan Williamson, and Paddy Houlahan and his Gypsy Musicians.

I am particularly indebted to the following:
Peter Kennedy's Folktracks collection at Brunswick Square, Gloucester
Early in the Month of Spring, issued by Pat Mackenzie and Jim Carol with the
English Folk Dance and Song Society
The collection of songs made by Gwillwm and Carol Davies.

Books I have found especially helpful are:
Twelve Traditional Carols from Herefordshire by Ralph Vaughan Williams and
Ella Mary Leather (Stainer 1920)
The Folklore of Herefordshire by Ella Mary Leather (Lapridge 1991)
A Nest of Singing Birds by Lavender Jones (published privately 1978)
Folk Songs of Britain and Ireland by Peter Kennedy (Cassell 1975)
The Romano Drom Song Book (Romanestan Publications)

My transcriptions of the songs give the individual versions of the songs as I heard them. Most of the songs are traditional, but in some cases the composers are known, so where an actual composer is noted, that song is still in copyright.

Romani has only recently become a written language and spellings vary. For words which have been Anglicised we have used the Romani spellings.

Many of the songs in this book can be heard on a companion cassette *Songs from the Roadside* available from the publishers or from Romany Records, Hatfield Court, near Leominster.

I have received generous support for this project from BBC Hereford and Worcester and West Midlands Arts.

J.S.

ILLUSTRATIONS

IN 1912, the composer Ralph Vaughan Williams was asked by a newspaper man what had been his most memorable musical impression for the year. He replied that it was hearing a Gypsy sing at Monkland, the picturesque village a few miles from Leominster.

He'd gone with Ella Mary Leather, a solicitor's wife from Castle House, Weobley, who often took Vaughan Williams and his wife on visits to friends of hers who were Gypsies. After some false starts, they found the Gypsy camp in a little round field at dusk. It was evening, after a long day's hop picking. There were several caravans, each with its wood fire burning.

The Gypsy Harriet Jones was there with some of her fifteen children, and Alfred Price Jones, probably her father. Alfred's wife was ill and he was sitting with her under an awning near one of the fires. He agreed to sing and, says Ella Mary Leather,

> We all sat down on upturned buckets, kindly provided for us by the Gypsies. While Dr Vaughan Williams noted down the tune his wife and I noted down alternate lines of the words.
>
> It is difficult to convey to those who have never known it the joy of hearing folk songs as we heard that ballad; the difference between hearing it there and in a drawing room or concert hall is just that between discovering a wild flower growing in its native habitat and admiring it when transplanted to a botanical garden.

Vaughan Williams himself wrote,

> It was a cold, clear September night and we were by the blazing fire in the open ground of the Gypsy encampment; the fire had been specially lighted to enable us to note down tunes and words in the growing darkness.

1

Then out of the half-light came the sound of a beautiful tenor voice, singing 'The Unquiet Grave'.

'Cold blows the wind for my true love,
Cold blows the drops of rain,
I never, never had but one true love,
And in green wood he was slain.

I'll do as much for my true love,
As any young girl may,
For I will sit and weep down by the grave,
For twelve months and a day.'

When twelve months and a day were gone,
This young man he arose;
'Why do you weep down by my grave,
That I can take no repose?

O fetch me a nut from a dungeon deep,
Or water out of a stone.
Or white, white milk from a fair maid's breast,
Or from me begone.'

'How can I fetch a nut from a dungeon deep,
Or water out of a stone;
Or white, white milk from a fair maid's breast,
When fair maid she is none?'

'If you have one kiss from my lily white lips
Your days will not be long,
My lips are as cold as any clay,
My breath it is earthy and strong.'

> *'One kiss, one kiss from your lily white lips*
> *One kiss from you I crave.'*
> *'The cock does crow and we must part,*
> *I must return to my grave.'*

Ralph Vaughan Williams made many other expeditions into the world of our Herefordshire Gypsies and other traditional English singers, bringing back priceless words and melodies that he incorporated into his music. Two of the melodies in his *Fantasia on Christmas Carols* came from Herefordshire Gypsies, and in 1920, with Ella Mary Leather, he published *Twelve Traditional Carols from Herefordshire*. Of these carols he got at least nine from our Herefordshire Gypsies. Many were recorded by Ella and others on cylinder at The Homme, the well known hop farm near Weobley, where many Gypsy families used to camp in those days.

One of these ancient carols was 'On Christmas Day It Happened So', sung by Esther Smith at the Homme and which, so it has been claimed, is unique; it has never been recorded from any other source.

Vaughan Williams changed the words when he published it. The original tells how a ploughman goes to plough on Christmas Day. Suddenly Jesus appears beside him and asks why he's ploughing on God's birthday. He must, says the ploughman; 'for to plough this day we have great need.' The outcome is most unexpected:

> *His arms did quaver, he could not plough,*
> *The ground did open and loose him in.*

And, sang Esther Smith, he's not the only one in his family on whom falls a terrible retribution:

> *His wife and children are out of place*
> *His beasts and cattle they die away.*

It is possible that Esther Smith may have got particular satisfaction that this man was a farmer because although for centuries farmers had been the Travellers' traditional benefactors, allowing them to camp on their land, they were also their exploiters, relying on them to work efficiently and hard at harvest time for low wages.

> *On Christmas Day it happened so,*
> *Down in the meadows for to plough;*
> *As we were ploughing on so fast,*
> *Up comes sweet Jesus his self at last.*
>
> *'O man! O man! what makes you plough*
> *So hard upon the Lord's birthday?'*
> *The farmer answered him with great speed,*
> *'For to plough this day we have great need.'*
>
> *His arms did quaver to and fro,*
> *His arms did quaver he could not plough,*
> *The ground did open and loose him in,*
> *Before he could repent of sin.*
>
> *His wife and children are out of place,*
> *His beasts and cattle they die away,*
> *His beasts and cattle they die away,*
> *For the breaking of our Lord's birthday.*

At first the Gypsies had been shy and suspicious of Ella Mary Leather. Ella bribed one of the younger women, Angelina Whatton, with a present of a silk blouse, and at length she sang 'Under the Leaves'. This is a carol of great antiquity dating in part back to the fifteenth century.

Angelina's mother and Mrs Loveridge then sang the carol as well, each with small variations. Mrs Loveridge was a keeper's daughter from Stoke Edith, perhaps on the Foley estate. Gifted with a beautiful voice, she had run away to marry a Gypsy to whom she bore nine children.

Wonderfully strong on melody, quite astonishing in their imagery, and belonging more to the world of the Old Testament than to the New, these are sacred Christian songs, sung by people with a deep and unquestioning faith; but underneath we seem to be reeling on the edge of something else.

Under the leaves, the leaves of life
There saw I maidens to seven,
And one of them was Mary mild
As was our King's Mother from heaven.

They asked me what I was looking for
All under the leaves of life;
'I am looking for sweet Jesus Christ
With his body nailed to a tree.'

'Go you down, go you down to yonder town
As far as the Holy Well,
And there you'll find sweet Jesus Christ
With his body nailed to a tree.'

'Dear Mother, do not weep for me,
Your weeping does me some harm,
That John may be a comfort to you,
When I am dead and gone.

'Dear mother, dear mother, you must love John,
For John is an angel so bright,
That he may be a comfort to you
When I am dead and gone.'

'Oh no, dear Son, that never can be,
That I should love John
As well as my own Son Jesus,
That I bore from my own body.'

Oh the rose, the rose, the genteel rose,
The fern that grows so green,
May the Lord give us grace in every place,
For to pray till our ending day.

Vaughan Williams adored the tunes but he didn't always appreciate the richness of the words of the Gypsy carols. He tidied them up. A carol sung by Angelina Whatton goes:

Christ made a trance one Sunday view,
All with his own dear hands,
He made the sun clear all off the moon,
Like the water off dry land.

Is this speaking of an eclipse, I wonder, or is it an ancient creation myth? Here's how Vaughan Williams dealt with it:

> God in the Holy Trinity
> All with his mighty hand
> Hath made the sun, the stars, the moon
> The water and dry land.

All very worthy, but rather routine Edwardian stuff.

Sung by Angelina Whatton the song also contains the extraordinary:

> *Oh, hell is deep and hell is dark*
> *And hell is full of moss;*

Moss may be short for remorse. Another explanation may be that the word moss is used by Gypsies to mean waste boggy land, or useless heath land, good for nothing, not even for grazing a horse; and maybe they felt there was a lot of that in hell. This image, whatever its exact meaning, was not allowed by Ralph Vaughan Williams.

Ella Mary Leather wrote of this song,

All the Gypsies who have sung for me know the carol, and the usual version had 'Sunday view' in the first line; none could explain what the first verse meant. [It] is probably a corruption of something quite different in meaning. The extraordinary image of the sun clearing all off the moon, like the water off dry land, may be a survival of a pre-Christian creation myth.

Christ made a trance one Sunday view,
All with his own dear hands,
He made the sun clear all off the moon,
Like the water off dry land.

Like the water off the land, man Christ,
What died upon the Cross;
What shall we do for our Saviour,
As he has done for us?

What shall we do for our Saviour, man Christ,
What died upon the Cross?
We'll do as much for you, dear Lord
As you have done for us.

Oh, hell is deep and hell is dark
And hell is full of moss;
What shall we do for our Saviour
That he has done for us?

Oh, these six days in all this week,
Are for the labouring man,
And the seventh for to serve the Lord
Both the Father and the Son.

Come, teach your children well, dear man,
And teach them when they're young,
The better it'll be for your own dear soul,
When you are dead and gone.

The holy family ride in splendour in some of these old songs; but there are others in which they are thoroughly domestic, rather like Gypsies. Gypsies at Sutton St Nicholas used this fragment from a longer song to sing about how Jesus asked his mother if he could go out to play:

> *As it fell out on my holiday,*
> *As my holiday so wide,*
> *Sweet Jesus he asked of his own Mother dear*
> *Whether he should go to play.*
>
> *'To play, to play, dear child,' she did say,*
> *'It's time that you was being gone,*
> *And don't let me hear no complaint upon you*
> *At night when you do came home.'*

Perhaps the most extraordinary of all these sacred songs, sung at The Homme by Esther and Eliza Smith, was this:

> *There is a fountain of Christ's blood*
> *Wide open shed to drown our sins,*
> *Where Jesus stands with open arms*
> *Of mercy to invite you in.*
>
> *When all his precious blood was spent,*
> *The sea did roar, the rocks were rent,*
> *The earth did quake and clouds did rumble,*
> *Which made earth shake and devils tremble.*

The sun and moon in mourning went,
The sea did roar, the rocks were rent,
There you may see his bleeding wounds,
And hear him bring forth dying groans.

He shed his rich redeeming blood
Only to do poor sinners good.

Vaughan Williams gave this song different words in the version he published, and it is with these different words that it has been recorded by the choir of King's College, Cambridge. He also produced a version for tenor and piano and, as it gets further from the fields and closer to the drawing room and concert hall, the Gypsy song changes its nature. I like to honour all types of music, and the song as sung by Esther and Eliza Smith is so fine it can survive any number of interpretations. Myself, I agree with Mrs Leather; it's the difference between hearing it in a concert hall and hearing it in the wild; between a cultivated flower growing in a drawing room or botanical hothouse, and a flower growing wild found unexpectedly in a Herefordshire meadow.

The famous melody of the hymn 'He who would valiant be' was taken from 'The Blacksmith', another song Vaughan Williams got from these parts, sung for him by Harriet Jones, amongst others, at The Homme. The original words are different to those used by Vaughan Williams:

For a blacksmith he courted me, both late and yarly
Until he won my heart, wrote to me a letter
With his hammer in his hand, strikes his blows so neat and clever
And if I were with my love, I'd live for ever.

Now he talks about going abroad, fighting for strangers
And he'd better stay at home, and keep from all dangers;
For you stay at home with me, my dearest jewel
And you stay at home with me, and don't prove cruel.

My true love's gone across the sea, gathering fine posies
My true love's gone across the sea, with his cheeks like roses;
I'm afraid that broiling sun will spoil his beauty
And if I was with my love, I would do love's duty.

For it's once I had gold in store, they all seemed to like me
And now I'm low and poor, they all seem to slight me;
For there ain't no belief in a man, nor your own brother
So it's: Girls, whenever you love, love one each other.

As well as the singers there were in the early years of this century many Gypsy players on the fiddle. The Locke family, also
known as the Gentlemen Lockes, travelled the West Midlands
with twenty or thirty donkeys in scarlet harness and were
renowned for their skill at fiddle playing. And does any memory
remain of the music of these Lockes, still living in this area on
Council sites and lay-bys and in houses?

Yes, one cylinder remains in the vaults of the English Folk
Dance and Song Society. This stylish rendering of the 'Three Jolly
Black Sheepskins' is the sound that made hearts beat the stronger
eighty years ago: the actual music of the man who, if he called
at a pub, would find that his cider had been laced with spirits
and his bow primed with bacon fat so he would get out his fiddle
and play on, never stop. And to whose bender tent presents of
vegetables and eggs were brought to encourage him to play.

In the dance of the 'Three Jolly Black Sheepskins', three fleeces are placed on the floor of the pub. The dancers perform an intricate step dance around them. If you put a foot wrong the next round is on you.

Ella Mary Leather had met John Locke in Pembridge in 1908, and became friendly with him and his family. Thereafter, when visiting her in Weobley, he announced his arrival by playing under her window. Once a number of Lockes arrived as Ella was giving a party. The maid tried to turn them away but Ella appeared and invited them in to join the party, to the great surprise of some of the guests. Mrs Locke once arrived to see Ella and was told by a maid that she couldn't come in because Mrs Leather was upstairs having a siesta. The Gypsy asked for a sheet of paper and the maid, thinking she wanted to write a message, brought one. Mrs Locke tore it into little pieces, put one piece in each corner of her basket and a series of pieces along Ella's doorstep and window sills. The maid was terrified and, as soon as the Gypsy woman was gone, swept up all the pieces of paper.

'You can never mistake a Locke, they are so long,' Ella was told.

John Locke was later found tragically dead in the snow on the Long Mynd, stretched out with his violin beside him.

The days of greatest prosperity for many British Gypsies was in the last hundred years of the great days of the horse, when a travelling Gypsy horse-dealing family might be accompanied by a hundred horses. The affluence following from horse dealing enabled some Gypsies to build up the small fortunes necessary to commission the brilliant caravan waggons in which they travelled.

Where did they come from? One legend has it that in Pakistan a thousand years ago Gypsies were the camp followers of an immense army. They were the tinsmiths and cooks, the makers of arms, providers of charms and remedies for the wounded, cooks, performers, singers, dancers. The army was bloodily wiped out in a cataclysmic territorial battle; and the Gypsies, with nowhere to go, have been wandering west ever since, bringing with them many riches to the countries along their route—camping, caravans, tents, horse racing, circus, herbal remedies, fortune telling; and perhaps most important of all, a concept of the romantic. Romani romantic has come to stand for many things the world finds deliciously full of romance, plus a touch of frisson.

Music too. Well known is Raya, the Rumanian Gypsy singer said to have been discovered at the age of six, orphaned, wandering round the ruins of a war shattered Berlin. Many people have remarked on the crucial place of Gypsies in East European and especially Hungarian music. The composer Liszt claimed that the famous national music of Hungary had been created by its Gypsy citizens. Above the title of his 'Nineteen Hungarian Rhapsodies', he wrote 'Hungarians have accepted the Gypsies as their National Musicians.' In these Rhapsodies he sought, he said, to transcribe the music of those Gypsy musicians he heard playing on his visits to Hungary. He was 'quite absorbed by the warlike fervour and the deep sorrow of Gypsy music...couched in an unusual language and form, unusual as everything Gypsy is unusual.'

Others came to qualify Liszt's claims, but it's hard to deny Gypsies their central place in the music of Hungary and many other countries, especially Russia, and Spain, home of Manitas de Plata, the great Gypsy flamenco guitarist and singer from Andalucia. It's thought that Gypsies brought an early form of this flamenco across the Straits of Gibraltar from Morocco as their musical gift to Spain, and their many services to Spain were recently honoured in Seville when Gypsies from all the countries of the European Union, including some sixty from Britain, were guests at a conference opened by the Queen and closed by the President.

Gypsies are first recorded as being in these islands five hundred years ago. The Gypsy Johnny Farr and his troupe were befriended by James V of Scotland. They sang and danced for him at Holyrood Palace for which they were given a handsome reward and a safe conduct for Scotland. A ballad, 'Johnny Farr', records how Lady Cassilis, a real woman, left castle, Lord, family, everything, to run away with Johnny Farr and the Gypsies.

Later King and Gypsies fell out. Some say the King made a pass at one of the Gypsy women—always a dangerous thing to do with Gypsies.

Just as in the case of King James, few people today are neutral about the Gypsy nation. For a start, it's huge: eleven million worldwide, six million in the continent of Europe. Many non-Gypsy people find them hard to relate to, and are sometimes a little fearful, often even hostile; others, like myself, seem to go overboard, entranced by that famous Gypsy glamour.

My grandmother, Mary Carbery, was one of the fans, a Romani speaker, travelling in a horse-drawn caravan from the windows of which at the age of six my father first saw Hereford-shire.

Later he settled near Leominster, bringing grandmother to spend her last decade in a cottage near his home, with her old caravan parked outside on the lawn; from her I early picked up a fascination for the Gypsies I saw camped on the roadside verges and commons of this county; and for those Gypsies who some-times looked in to see her, from one of whom she took lessons in Romani.

The names of the Gypsies from whom Vaughan Williams got such wonderful words and music were, among others, Mrs Johnson, Mrs Loveridge, William Colcombe, Angelina Whatton, her mother Mrs Whatton, David Price Jones, his daughter Harriet Jones, and Esther and Eliza Smith.

Do their descendants still live round here? I wondered. Since many of the recordings were made at The Homme, I decided to go there. It's a substantial square three storey brick building with oast houses, a typical well-to-do Herefordshire farmhouse, lying down narrow green verged lanes near Weobley. The owner of The Homme came to the top of the steps leading to his front door and regarded me warily. His name was John Pudge.

Oh yes, they always had plenty of Gypsies camped in the meadow up there, he said, in the days of his father, John Pudge, and his grandfather, also called John Pudge. Most farms today, of course, are mechanised; there's little call for the Gypsies' labour these days. Smiths? Whattons? John Pudge thought there were Gypsies of that name parked by the nearby main road, the A4112.

And down there by the road I found a number of spotless shiny Gypsy caravans, squashed into a narrow space at the corner of a field, enclosed by ten-foot high wire mesh fences put there by the Council. All along the road the ample greenswards and verges, the traditional stopping places for Travellers, had been ditched, wired off, or otherwise blocked by officialdom.

Inside these caravans, with their immaculate Nottingham lace curtains, green and gold shell cushions, glint of dark blue and gold of Crown Derby, caravans whose very names are exotic— Weippart, Buccaneer, Roma—would I find descendants of Loveridge, Johnson, Locke, Whatton? Esther and Eliza Smith?

'Yes,' Evelyn Smith told me, 'my husband Harry's grandmother was born Esther Whatton and she became Esther Smith when she married. So she was sister-in-law to Eliza Smith. Harry's grandmother was Esther Smith and mine was Eliza.'

Harry & Evelyn Smith

v'95

In the course of conversation with Harry and Evelyn, most of the other names of Vaughan Williams' singers cropped up as relatives. Gypsies do not as a general rule approve of their children marrying non-Gypsies, and there has been much intermarriage between the great Herefordshire Gypsy families.

It was hard not to notice in passing that these people, so smartly dressed, so dignified, so clean and tidy, and their bevies of immaculate children, were crammed into a small space without drainage or mains electricity, children's play space, men's work space, or running water. They get their water in milk churns from the nearest public tap, six miles away, the other side of Dinmore.

My reading of government guidelines, European law and the Children Act is that our council is out of order here. Councils must seek out children in need in their areas and provide basic amenities. That, however, is another story, albeit an all too typical Herefordshire story.

In a small house in nearby Weobley I talked to Eliza Smith, a granddaughter through marriage of Esther Smith. She certainly could sing the old songs, she told me:

> My Dan used to play the accordion and my one uncle he had a harp and my sisters used to play too, divine, beautiful. Them all has passed away. I wonder what became of the harp? That harp has vanished. I was very upset about that. We used to go to Appleby and to Stow Fair and to Nottingham Fair. You'd like it. Goose Fair is very nice. Martly Green Fair in Shropshire that's been going for a thousand years, it's more for horses, beautiful horses, 'cos there's a lot of our people still goes with the culture. Misfortunately I haven't been this last couple of years.
>
> We used to have good times hopping, good times. Now all the good things is took away from us. Free as a bird we used to be. I wish it would all come back. Sad times now. Not so friendly.

Eliza said she'd be glad to sing for me but she couldn't that day. She'd only just got back from an operation in hospital and was still breathless. Would I come back in a week or two?

I called round a few weeks later. Many Gypsies thronged the street outside Eliza's home. There was a Gypsy funeral about to take place. Eliza Smith's funeral. God bless her.

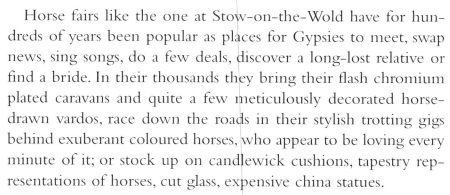

Horse fairs like the one at Stow-on-the-Wold have for hundreds of years been popular as places for Gypsies to meet, swap news, sing songs, do a few deals, discover a long-lost relative or find a bride. In their thousands they bring their flash chromium plated caravans and quite a few meticulously decorated horse-drawn vardos, race down the roads in their stylish trotting gigs behind exuberant coloured horses, who appear to be loving every minute of it; or stock up on candlewick cushions, tapestry representations of horses, cut glass, expensive china statues.

Here you can hear present-day Gypsy music and, although they still sing the old songs, strong favourites these days are the Irish and Scottish jigs and reels and waltzes, music that works like whisky. If this music lacks a certain continental sensuality and complexity, then it amply makes up for it by its intoxicating transformation of any environment into an instant party.

Even more important than Irish and Scottish music to today's Gypsies is Country and Western. Many of the songs I heard at Stow are not original to Gypsies. But a very special transformation takes place in any song when it is sung by a Gypsy. There is a deep injection of heart, a deep knowledge of life in all its vagaries.

You're like a dream
Of peaches and cream
And lips like strawberry wine,
You're beautiful,
You're sixteen,
And you're mine!

The Bell public house, next to the horse fair, is packed and outside it I join a group of Gypsy singers, twenty of them, standing round in a circle. Like everyone here they're dressed up to the nines, the men in shirts so bright they shine, women show quite a lot of bosom and above all bare midriff, recalling the Asian sub-continent from which their ancestors came long ago.

We fell in love on the night we met
You touched my hand
And ooh when we kissed
I could not stop!

Twice a year the antique shop owners of this mellow honey-coloured town are shaken out of their complacent dreams amid their antique furniture and rural painting behind plate glass windows. And by what a festivity! The streets are crammed with folk, the women dressed with such care and exoticism that the initial feeling is they're on their way to a ball, a ball at midday.

There is a fair display of the gold that worldwide is so important to Gypsies, multiple gold chains and talismanic ornaments hang round honey-coloured shoulders, or the clothes themselves are sewn or shot through with sequins or gold thread. Some women wear their hair in a beehive. Traditional Gypsy women do not show their legs, but some here wear lace or hoisted-up skirts, showing hot pants or a long length of thigh.

The men, casually dressed with chunky sweaters over shirts sometimes unbuttoned far down the chest, baggy trousers, expensive fancy leather shoes, look, as is often none less than the case, as if at any moment they must be ready to demonstrate their equestrian ability by jumping on the back of a horse. The many coloured horses, piebald and skewbald, look around from the stakes and hedges to which they're tethered with wise toler-ance. They've seen it all before.

> *You walked out of my dreams*
> *And into my arms*
> *Now you're my angel divine*
> *Your're sixteen,*
> *You're beautiful,*
> *And you're mine!*

In the deep muddy gulf that runs through the middle of this fair, cars and lorries crammed with bevies of exquisite young women and sombre young men, getting stuck, wheels spinning in the mud, are weaving their slippery way back up the hillside and sometimes making it. Gypsy men fight, for prize money or to settle a disagreement, stripped to the waist, watched by scores of spectators. There are also fights between exotically ballgown-dressed lovelies; one of which spills out of the fair, past the pub, and up to the town, the police trying to keep them apart and finally holding one woman by the arm and marching her off, she still turning back to shout insults at the women behind.

A guitarist, singer and melodion player, George Smith is a frequent visitor to Stow Fair:

Travellers like country music because they can sing country music and country music goes back a long way. When you think of today, the nineties, you put the wireless on, all you hear is the background, you hear no voice, even if you do you can't make no sense out of it. I mean, I've had the wireless on today and I've druv about two hundred and fifty mile today and every bit of it hasn't made a blind bit of sense to me.

I think country music, Boxcar Willy, Johnny Cash, Jimmy Rogers (and that goes back a long way, old Jimmy Rogers) and old Slim Whitman, Frank Ifield, people can understand that.

You listen to the singer, the voice is coming out of the singer, and that's why Travellers likes it.

As life on the road becomes harder and more and more Gypsies are forced off the roads and into houses, so the importance of horse fairs like this, to endorse and re-establish Gypsy identity and heritage, becomes the more crucial.

Like most of the traditional Gypsy Travellers whose caravans are parked in lay-bys and by our busy trunk roads, George's family have been living in the West Midlands for generations.

I was born at Symond's Yat, that's about thirty miles from here, I was born in a tent. My mother always said to me, anybody was born in a tent would grow up, look healthy, and get on better, and I think she's right because, I mean, I think I'm all right.

They had the horse drawn caravans then. As time went on they kept to the times, you know, done away with the horses, bought the lorries.

There's been change in other areas besides the move from tents and caravans to trailers, horses to lorries. As many as half our Gypsy population have been forced, often against their will, to move into flats and houses. The Irishman Paddy Houlahan and his Gypsy musicians, in a song admired by many British Gypsies, uses the idiom to reflect on a perennial Gypsy predicament: what happens to those Gypsies who sell their caravan and birthright, and move into a flat?

My father rises early
And makes a sup of tea,
He lights the kitchen stove
And then he calls me.
His days are often empty
Nothing much to do,
So he tells me stories
Of the travelling life he knew.

In the evening they would meet
In lonely country lanes,
A field away you'd hear a collie bark
And they'd pass the time away
With talk about the day,
Standing round the campfire in the dark,
Standing round the campfire in the dark.

My mother likes the house,
The hot water and the rooms,
It's warm in the winter
And she's handy with the broom.

Sometimes she makes colcannon,
More often griddled bread,
But there's a hunger deep inside her
For a life that's nearly dead.

In the evening she would lift
The black pot from the coals
'A bit too late', she always would remark.
There'd be vessels left to clean,
Wild children could be seen,
Playing round the campfire in the dark,
Playing round the campfire in the dark.

We go down to the pool hall
And chat up this town of yours;
Sometimes at a disco
We can't get past the doors.
We're still tinkers to them,
It's thrown at our ears;
We're still the strangers
After all these years.

I think about my own life,
The way that it will be,
An Escort van, a bit of dealing
A wife and a family.
Thursday I collect the dole,
Maybe pitch and toss,
On the site I think about
The Travellers' ways we've lost.

And I wish that I could rise
And wash the sleep out of my eyes,
Listening to the sweet song of the lark.
And I wish I could be
Of that campfire company,
With the sound of horses moving in the dark,
With the sound of horses moving in the dark.

Other idioms, rock, pop, house, are to be heard at Gypsy weddings, wakes, and other gatherings, but it is to country music that they these days most often return for themselves.

Houlahan reflects on another Gypsy predicament: how to relate to the house-dwelling population. 'But I knew the farmer,' says another of his songs, 'I traded him a mare,' recalling the days when Gypsies were in high demand as a cheap and efficient mobile labour force, very useful in time of harvest. These days, says Houlahan, things have changed. Gypsies have become 'invisible'.

The books you read at school
Do not mention me,
Because I am the Invisible Man
In this country's history.

But I knew the farmer,
I traded him a mare,
I picked his beet and shaped his tins
And I was welcome there.

Now, however, says Houlahan, there's

No more call for my trade
Everything's plastic made,
No more travelling around.
I'm living on the edge of your town.

I see the way you feel
Reflected in your eyes;
One hard look is all it took
To make me realise
That you are afraid of me
Though you don't know my name.
But if something's done by anyone
I must take the blame.

By the ashes of a fire at Stow Fair at dawn, a lonely Stow Fair, so many folks are asleep in caravans or tents, and so late at night it's turned into the morning, Mark O'Gallaidhe sings one of the most popular of all Gypsy songs. Every moment of every day, some Gypsy will be singing it somewhere. To hear this song, not at all in the Country and Western tradition, is like looking under the reflective glitter of water into the depths underneath, to the tradition that comes very much from our own heritage, from these islands:

I'm a Romani Rai
I'm a young didikai
I travel the roads with me dog and me grai.
I don't pay no rent
'Cos I live in a tent
And that's why they call me
The Romani Rai.

Dikka chavvi, dik akai
Dikka chavvi, dik akai
Daddy's trying to sell the mush a kushti grai,
Kakka chavvi, dik akai,
Kakka chavvi, dik akai,
That's why they call me
The Romani Rai.

I'm a Romani Rom
I travel the drom
I hawk all the day and I dance through the night,
I'll never grow rich
I was born in a ditch
And that's why they call me
The Romani Rai.

I'm a Romani Rai
I'm a true didikai
I make willow creels, on the bosh play the reels
I'll sing you a song
'Fore the gavvers gell me on,
And that's why they call me
The Romani Rai.

Rai in Romani means a lord or gentleman, so this is a song about being a free spirit, a Gypsy gentleman. The chorus, Dikka chavvi, Dik akai, means 'hush, baby, hush', and the next line; 'Daddy's trying to do a deal with a man about a kushti grai, a handsome horse.'

The most poignant line of all for me is 'I'll sing you a song 'fore the gavvers move me on'. Gavver is a police officer and this for me is about the fragile joy of our Gypsies, the fragile moment of spontaneity before the forces of house-dwelling officialdom come in once again to move them from farm or verge or common, back among the traffic on the road.

There is no sadness in this song. In 'I'm a Freeborn Man', another popular celebration of the travelling life, adapted by Ewan McColl from a Gypsy original, there is in the last verse a momentary acknowledgement of what it calls the 'winds of change'.

I'm a freeborn man of the travelling people,
Got no fixed abode, with nomads I am numbered;
Country lanes and by-ways were always my ways,
I never fancied being lumbered.

Oh we knew the woods and the resting places
And the small bird sang when winter days were over;
Then we'd pack our load and be on the road,
Those were good old times for a rover.

There was open ground where a man could linger
For a week or two, for time was not our master;
Then away you'd jog with your horse and dog,
Nice and easy, no need to go faster.

Now and then you'd meet up with other travellers
Hear the news, or else swop family information;
At the country fairs, you'd be meeting there
All the people of the travelling nation.

Now I've known life hard and I've known it easy,
And I've cursed that life when winter days were dawning;
But we've laughed and sung through the whole night long,
Seen the summer sun rise in the morning.

All you freeborn men of the travelling people,
Every tinker, rolling stone and gypsy rover,
Winds of change are blowing, old ways are going;
Your travelling days may soon be over.

Earthy, redolent of our meadows and trees and Gypsy people, is the forthright gay song of a young lass who's just reached puberty, sung by the Gypsy Mary Delaney, currently living in a caravan in Birmingham.

As she happily tells us, she's young and she's airy, and bold contrary, and buckled she longs to be. Her mother feels she is too young and offers various diversions which also will be a source of income so she will be independent. But no, the daughter is far too young and airy and bold contrary for anything like that. So finally her mother says she'll get her a man! Now you're talking, says the daughter:

'I was fourteen years last Sunday, Mamma, I'm longing for to be wed,
In the arms of some young man'd comfort me in bed,
In the arms of some young man would roll with me all night,
I'm young and I'm airy and bold contrary and buckled I'd long to be.'

'Hold your tongue, dear daughter,' she says, 'I was forty when I was
    wed,
And as it was no shame for me to carry me boss into bed.'
'For if that was the way with you, Mamma, it is not the way with me,
I'm young and I'm airy and bold contrary and buckled I'd like to be.'

'Hold your tongue, dear daughter,' she says, 'And I will buy you a sheep.'
'No indeed, Mamma,' she says, 'That would cause me for to weep,
To weep and weep and weep, Mamma, it's a thing I never can do.'
'For I'll send you down to the meadows all day and I'll stop you from
    drinking too.'

'Hold your tongue, dear daughter,' she says, 'And I will buy you a cow.'
'No indeed, Mamma,' she says, ' 'Twould cause me for to vow,
To vow, to vow and vow, Mamma, that's a thing I never will do.
I'm young and I'm airy and cracked and contrary and buckled I'd long
    to be.'

'Hold your tongue, dear daughter,' she says, 'And I will buy you a man.'
'Do indeed, dear Mother,' she says, 'For the sooner the better you can,
For if that is the way with you, Mamma, it is not the way with me.
I'm young and I'm airy and bold contrary and buckled I'd like to be.'

Some of these songs come from a unique Gypsy tradition and some from the British tradition that we all shared once. It may well be that our Gypsies are the only English people still sitting together of an evening, still singing songs passed down from mother to daughter and grandfather to grandson.

'My Old Horse and Me' by Duncan Williamson looks back with nostalgia to the days of the horse. Although a new song, it's very exactly a part of that ancient tradition.

O the summer time is come again
But it surely breaks my heart
When I think of the happy days I spent
With my old horse and cart.

For the roads they were not long for him
Nor yet too long for me,
It's on the road I used to go
Of my old horse and me.

O many's the time on a winter's night
He stood tied to a tree
With no' a bite to give to him
Or no' a bite for me.

With a wee bit cover across his back
To shelter him from the snow
And I know it's in the morning
On the road I'd have to go.

O many's a time upon the road
My old horsey lost a shoe,
Up to the smithy I would go
To the smithy man I'd view.

'I cannae buy a new shoe'
To the smithy man I'd say,
'O put me on an old one
I'm sure it will last today.'

Now, those happy days are gone past
I've bought a motor car,
Sure I go drivin' on those roads
I'm sure I travel far.

I drive past all those places
But I'll turn to you and say,
I'll never be as happy as I was
With my old horse and me.

For those roads they were not long for him
Nor yet too long for me,
It's on those roads I used to go
Of my old horse and me.

The West Midlands are not that far from Liverpool and the ferries, and Irish Travellers come over here periodically and some make this country their home. One of the most enigmatic of Gypsy songs concerns something quite dreadful which occurred somewhere named Ballaroo in Ireland. The song puts the story into the mouth of a 'poor old man', the unwitting witness of terrible events.

Some time ago in County Wexford, the story goes, the respected Gypsy horse-dealing family of Connors fell out with another Gypsy family called the Moorhouses. The Connors took to their fists, there was a fight in the town square and the Connors got the worst of it. The tribe went running out of town.

The Connors barricaded themselves in an abandoned cottage. The Moorhouses climbed on the roof, tore off the straw, and jumped down on to the Connors. The Connors were trapped.

The song is sung by Johnny 'Pops' Connors, who has spent much of his life in a caravan in the Birmingham area. What happened to them all, I wonder? The mists of history open just for a minute to disclose this awful event in Ballaroo, then close again as abruptly as they opened.

> *How di dowden diddle di aye*
> *Di di andie diddle di aye*
> *Dattle se old dey di sahm*
> *Bye di aye tidie ay.*
>
> *'What brought you down from Kerry?'*
> *Says the poor old man.*
> *'Sure it's the Connors as is to blame*
> *And don't the country know the same,*
> *And look at them running down that lane'*
> *Says the poor old man.*
>
> *'Bad luck to you, young Gerry'*
> *Says the poor old man,*
> *'If you cook a stew*
> *You don't cook it near Ballaroo,*
> *If you do, you're bound sure rue,'*
> *Says the poor old man.*

E didie nah di doodle didie
Vie die di da
Nah di deedle dar di dah
Do de deedie die di dah
Die di door en dum.

'Oh they were coming through Ross town
And they had ponies big and brown
And at me they did lick'
Says the poor old man.

'Bad luck to you, young Gerry'
Says the poor old man,
'I run to take my stick
And I got orders to drop it quick;
I'll not, I'll roar and squeal'
Says the poor old man.

'Bad luck to you, young Gerry'
Says the poor old man,
'But wasn't I an unlucky whore
To barricade my door?
Wasn't I an unlucky whore?'
Says the poor old man.

If something important happens, make a song about it. We were all doing it once, and the Gypsies are among the few English people still doing it in our own times. Ewan McColl has adapted this song from a Gypsy original:

The old ways are changing, you cannot deny,
The day of the traveller's over,
There's nowhere to go and there's nowhere to bide,
So farewell to the life of the rover.

Farewell to the tent and the old caravan,
To the tinker, the gypsy, the travelling man,
Farewell to the life of the rover.

Farewell to the cant and the travelling tongue,
Farewell to the Romani talking,
The buying and selling, the old fortune telling,
The knock at the door and the hawking.

You've got to move fast to keep up with the times,
For these days a man cannot dander,
There's a by-law to say you must be on your way,
And another to say you can't wander.

Farewell to the besoms of heather and broom,
Farewell to the creel and the basket,
The folks of today they would far sooner pay
For a thing that's been made out of plastic.

Farewell to the pony, the cob and the mare,
The reins and the harness are idle,
You don't need a strap when you're breaking up scrap,
So farewell to the bit and the bridle.

Many Gypsies were very willing to sing me their songs, but I was to learn that there are others who feel that the language, songs, customs, the whole culture, should not be shared with non-Gypsies, or Gorjios, as they call us.

'Don't Rocker to the Gorjios!', that is, don't speak with the house dwellers. Don't give them information or they may use it against you. 'Don't rocker to the Gorjios!' That's what Amos Smith's mother told him. Luckily, though, Amos is proud of his heritage and eager to tell me about it. He describes how the tarpaulin and long hazel ('bender') branches for the family tent were carried in those days on a flat topped waggon. Many Gypsies now in the prime of life were born in these bender tents. Even when there was a family horse-drawn waggon, in many families the pregnant mother built a new tent to give birth in. In the evening, after the bender tent had been erected by the roadside verge, the horse would be tethered to the shafts or a stake to nibble the verge; and possibly, later, sings Amos in a popular Gypsy jingle:

Mandi went to poove the grai
Down along the parni side
Up jumped a gaero
To low mandi's grai.
Mandi made a putch at 'im,
Hit him betwixt his snitch and chin,
Dordi Dordi Dordi
Can't mandi couer?

Amos Smith explains:

'Mandi' is I, went to graze the horse all along the 'parni side', that's the river side. 'Parni' is water. What we used to do, you're travelling along the road, so you pull in, on a bit of greensward, let the horse have a nibble, till it comes to eleven o'clock at night, tie him to the shafts or tie him to the back. And then, when it comes to eleven o'clock at night, 'Oh, it's all right now,' down to the gate, in what they call pooving the grai, in early next morning, fetch him out. 'Up jumps the gaero', the gaero is the man.

'Couer' means to fight, 'D'you want a couer?' means do you want a fight?

Years ago some of those old farmers used to be dead keen. And some of the coppers. Sometimes when you go to get the grai, sometimes the farmer's got up before they have! And when they go down to the field in the morning to get 'em at five o'clock, there's the farmer there waiting!'

As the old tradition of wandering is ever more curtailed, along with the Gypsies' customary right to camp on our commons and verges and greenswards, so the indestructible side of the Gypsy culture, the music, the language, becomes the more important to them, and some feel must not be made accessible to non-Gypsies. This must be respected. So, if I raise the tarpaulin an inch at the side of the tent of mysteries, only to let it fall, I hope that by gorjios, and Gypsies, I'll be forgiven.

Can you rokker Romani?
Can you feik the bosh?
Can you dik the vesher,
While mandi chins the kosh?

Can you talk in Romani?
Can you play the fiddle?
Can you spot the gamekeeper,
While I chop the wood?

Can you rokker Romani?
Can you poove a grai?
Can you chore a kanni,
While the mush is jelling by?

Can you talk in Romani?
Can you graze a horse?
Can you firkle a chicken?
As the farmer is going by?

Can you rokker Romani?
Can you dukker a rai?
Can you rokker Romesa,
And pukker as good as I?

Can you talk in Romani?
Can you tell a fortune?
Can you talk in Romani,
And chatter as good as I?

The musgros avved along one day,
To atch us on the drom,
But when they dikked how many
*   we was,*
They turned around and ran.

The policemen came along one day
To stop us on the road
But when they saw how many we
*   was,*
They turned around and ran.

I can pukker Romani,
I can feik the bosh.
I can dik a gavver mush,
While tuti chins the kosh.

I can talk in Romani
I can play the fiddle
I can spot a policeman,
While you chop the wood.

40

Wisdom 'Wiggy' Smith, the popular and accomplished traditional Gypsy singer who now lives on a council Gypsy caravan site not far from Tewkesbury, swigs copious draughts of old farm cider laced with whisky as he presides over a caravan filled with some ten of his seventy grandchildren and great grandchildren. Other friends and relatives drop in for a visit. He tells us of a useful Anglo-Romani approach for a man wanting to chat up a good looking woman; 'Kushti rackli, mandi wants to feik yer'. To which an appropriate reply, depending on inclination, might be; 'Kushti gaer, gell on wi' it!' This approach, however, should not be attempted by non-Gypsies.

Romani, he explains, is an expressive language:

It's like a horse is a grai, dog's a jukel, a faggot is a goat, chuchi is a rabbit, a poove is a field, or to graze a horse in a field, a grooki is a cow, a bolo is a pig, a mengri is a muskro, you name it mate, I can do it!

Wiggy gives us a brief introduction before singing us the ballad, the Oakham Poachers:

These Gypsies went out shooting one night, on a moonlit night, and then the keepers fired at 'em and that's what they called it the Oakham Poachers for, because the keepers shot at 'em and they fired back at the keepers, and that's why they called it the Oakham Poachers, it's an old tale from years ago. They killed the keeper, yes, they shot the keeper, and they went back and dug his eyes out afterwards, now you knows who I'm on about. They dug the eyes out because the Travellers said that they take the photograph out of the keeper's eyes of the one who shot him, and they went back and they dug his eyes out so they couldn't take the photograph and at the end it bothered 'em, got on their minds, you know, and they give themselves up, the two Travellers did, they both had life in prison and they both of them died in prison.

'Wiggy' Smith

43

It was on last February,
Against our laws conterary...

Off to Oakham Wood they rambled,
And among those briars and brambles;
And it's outside but near the centre,
Off into ambush they did lie.

These three brothers being brave hearted,
They boldly kept on firing;
Until one of them got the fateful blow
And it showed they was overthrown.

Off to Stafford gaol they then were taken,
And so cruelly were they beaten.
For it's in Stafford gaol they does now lie
Until their trial it does come on.

Now all you jolly poachers,
That does hear of we three brothers;
There is our brothers' sakes
Makes our heart ache
And they begged would us to die.

Highwaymen and even highwaywomen were a real menace in those days long ago before police cars. In another traditional English song sung by Wiggy Smith, it seemed a simple trip to the shops that she'd done hundreds of times before, but it was to have far reaching consequences for a certain young woman:

There was a rich farmer in Sheffield
And to market his daughter did go,
The daughter not being afraid though,
She's been on the Highway O before.

She met with three bold faced robbers
Three pistols they held at her breast,
The daughter not being afraid of,
She's been on the Highway O before.

The highwaymen strip the young woman naked to keep her valuable clothes and then, presumably while they wrap them up into a bundle which they can ride off with, one of them unwisely gives the naked girl his horse's reins to hold. But her rich father has evidently given her quite sophisticated riding lessons; suddenly she's leaped up on to the horse, riding it, not side-saddle, but astride like a man.

She put her left leg in their stirrup
And she mounted their horse like a man,
Over hedges and ditches she galloped
'Now come catch me, bold rogues, if you can.'

She rode back again to her father
And she shouted all over the farm,
'Dear father, I've been in great danger
But them rogues they 'aven't done me no harm.

Dear father, I've been in great danger
But these rogues 'aven't done me no harm!'
'And when you come to get married
I'll give you fifty thousand pounds, and more!'

What exactly took place on this extraordinary occasion? One of the intriguing things about traditional songs like this is that they themselves contain puzzles. Everyone knows the story already, so the singer is presenting a series of snapshots, not necessarily a complete story.

What actually seems to have happened is that in the saddle-bag on the highwayman's horse lay a vast stolen fortune. The father discovered this after his naked daughter had hurtled back into the farmyard so startlingly and dismounted. Both knew that any financial worries she might have had would now be a thing of the past.

Gypsies with their large families have provided many soldiers to fight and often to die in our wars, and life in an army at war may have been that much easier for Gypsies since they were used to living in the open. But with their strong tradition of autonomy, Gypsies have never been used to taking orders. They were frequently discriminated against and taunted, and a number have told how they always had to be ready with their fists. Gypsies are accustomed to living in large family units, with many women and children around, and when conscripted found it unsettling to be in exclusively male company, fighting for a country in which many citizens had little friendship to show them. The 'freedom' which soldiers are perennially told they are fighting for has, in the case of Gypsies, in time both of war and peace been fairly consistently eroded. Gypsies who could not read or write were not able to send news or receive it from home. When a telegram was finally delivered telling of a Gypsy soldier's death, it could be hard for their family to find anyone able to read it to them.

When on leave it could take Gypsy soldiers days to discover where their wives and children had got to. Prior to the First World War Gypsy dukkerers (fortune tellers) knew that something terrible was about to happen because they were perceiving catastrophe in the hands of so many of their male clients.

Some Gypsies inevitably considered ways in which they might escape the army, and the soldier in the song sung by Wiggy Smith that follows has feelings that are ambivalent.

The song is timeless, it is not even clear from the words whether it is his King or his Queen he would fight for.

I was once young and foolish, like many who is here;
I been fond of night rambling and I am fond of my beer.
Sure if I had my own home and my sweet liberty,
I would do no more soldiering, neither by land nor by sea.

Sure, the first time I deserted and I thought myself free,
I was quickly followed after and brought back by speed.
I was quickly followed after and brought back by speed,
And put in the Queen's guardroom, with heavy irons put on me.

You take off the heavy irons, and you let him go free,
For he'd make a brave soldier for his King and country.
You take off the heavy irons, and you let him go free
For he'll make a brave soldier for his Queen and country.

Sure if I had my own home and my sweet liberty,
I would do no more soldiering, neither by land nor by sea.

Tony Lloyd, a Gorjio growing up in Malvern, was entranced by the Gypsy families, Smith, Loveridge, and Whatton, camped in an orchard at the bottom of his parents' garden. He still sings the songs he learned then, including one about the murderer, Old Lankin, whose latest victim implores him:

'Old Lankin, O Lankin
Spare my life from your fire,
I'll fetch you my daughter Betsy
She's the sweetest of flowers.'

'What care I for your daughter Betsy
Or any of your kin?
She may hold a silver basin
For to catch your blood in.'

There's blood in the kitchen
There's blood in the hall
There's blood in the parlour
Where the lady did fall.

'Twas early next morning
Before break of day
When the maid she saw her master
Come a-riding that way.

'O master, O master,
Don't you lay the blame onto me,
Old Lankin he has murdered
Your Lady and her baby.'

'They have behind them not the imagination of one great poet, but the accumulated emotion, one may almost say, of the many successive generations who have read and learned and themselves fresh re-created the old majesty and loveliness ...

There is in them, as it were, the spiritual life blood of a people.'

Gilbert Murray wrote those words about the Bible and Homer, and for me they're also true of our own traditional songs and ballads.

Lacey Marie and Sabrina

Danny Brazil, a patriarch of the Brazil family once so famous for their singing, gave me a poignant insight into the world of a young Gypsy. He remembers, as a boy long ago with his brothers and sisters, lying in the family wagon in the cupboard bed under the master bed. They're parked on some greensward or meadow or common and they're listening, listening with their sharp ears, for the sound of distant singing...that would mean their parents were coming back, singing the old songs on their way back from the pub.

Evelyn Smith sits in her caravan on that tiny patch of land near Dilwyn, from which the farmer is planning to evict them:

> In ten years time there may not be any more Gypsies travelling around, they all will have been settled down. They'll be like Harry and me. We live in a caravan and we keep the old black pot and the kettle irons and the big black kettle, but apart from that they'll be more and more Gorjified.
>
> It's the travel being made so difficult these days. Also I think it's going to school. Travellers never used to go to school, but now they do and they pick up the Gorjio slang. My grandchildren are going to school and they learn to talk like Gorjios and they'll marry Gorjios and forty to fifty per cent of them will live in houses and take to Gorjio ways.
>
> Still, Gypsies are still very family people. A girl can't have a child with one man and then hitch up with another like the Gorjis do. She's got to make do with the one she's hitched up to.
>
> If a boy goes with a girl and she gets pregnant, he's got to marry her. Same with a girl. If you stop away with a boy for the night you've got to marry him. If you elope, then you've got to get married.

There are Gypsy girls who leave home and take up with Gorjio ways. It also happens the other way round, in reality and in songland. In a version of 'The Raggle Taggle Gypsies', sung by the Gypsy Mik Darling, the part of the Lady is poignantly sung by his daughter Susie. The Lord comes home, the servants tell him his wife has gone off with the Gypsies. He goes in search, and there she is:

O she's thrown away her high-heeled shoes
All made of Spanish leather O
And she would in the streets in her fair feet roam
All out in the wind and the weather O.

'O what makes you leave your house and land
What makes you leave all your money O
And what makes you leave your new-wedded Lord
To go with the Raggle Taggle Gypsies O?'

'O what care I for my house and land
What care I for my money O
And what care I for my new-wedded Lord?
I'm going with the Raggle Taggle Gypsies O.'

'O last night you slept in a goose feather bed
With the sheets turned down so bravely O
And tonight you'll sleep in an open field
Along with the Raggle Taggle Gypsies O.'

'Last night I slept in a goose feather bed
With the sheets turned down so bravely O
And tonight I'll sleep in an open field
Along with the Raggle Taggle Gypsies O.'

Another version of this ancient song tells of a similar incident, but with a different outcome. Although sometimes sung by

Gypsies it tells the story from a Gorjio point of view:

> *There came singers to Earl Cassilis' gate*
> *And O but they sang bonnie,*
> *They sang so sweet and so complete*
> *Till down came the Earl's lady.*
>
> *She came tripping down the stairs*
> *And all her maids before her,*
> *As soon as they saw her well-favoured face*
> *They cast their glamorie o'er her...*
>
> *They drunk her cloak, so did they her gown*
> *They drunk her stockings and her shoon,*
> *They drunk the coat was next to her stuck*
> *And they pawned her pearled apron.*
>
> *They were sixteen clever men*
> *Suppose they were nae bonny,*
> *They are all to be hanged on this day*
> *For the stealing of Earl Cassilis' lady.*

Many songs sung by Gypsies reveal their great antiquity. Others show the influence of the Victorian music hall. A Gypsy fortune-teller is surprised to recognise her future husband in the hand of the Gorjio man whose future she's foretelling. 'It is to be this little Gypsy girl,' she tells him excitedly and a trifle ingenuously, 'who is to be your bride!'

My father's the King of the Gypsies 'tis true
My mother she learned me some camping for to do
With my pack all on my back, my friends all wished me well
And I went up to London town some fortunes for to tell.

Some fortunes for to tell
Some fortunes for to tell
And I went up to London town some fortunes for to tell.

As I was a-walking through fair London's streets
A wealthy young Squire the first I chanced to meet
He viewed my brown cheeks and he liked them so well
Said he: 'My little Gypsy girl, can you my fortune tell?

Can you my fortune tell?
Can you my fortune tell?'
Said he: 'My little Gypsy girl, can you my fortune tell?'

'Oh yes,' replied the Gypsy girl, 'pray give me your hand
'Tis you that have good riches, both houses and good land,
The fairer girls are dainty but you must cast them by
For it is the little Gypsy girl that is to be your bride.

That is to be your bride,
That is to be your bride,
For it is the little Gypsy girl that is to be your bride.'

He took me to his palace, there were carpets on the floor
And servants there a-waiting for to open every door,
There were ladies there of honour and the music it did play
And all were there to celebrate the Gypsy's wedding day.

The Gypsy's wedding day,
The Gypsy's wedding day,
And all were there to celebrate the Gypsy's wedding day.

It's farewell to the Gypsy world and a-camping on the green
No more with my brothers or my sisters I'll be seen,
For I was a Gypsy girl but now I'm a Squire's bride
With servants for to wait on me and in my carriage ride.

And in my carriage ride,
And in my carriage ride,
With servants for to wait on me and in my carriage ride.

One Herefordshire Gypsy lass who married a Gorjio was the beautiful Esmeralda Locke. She left the tents, caravans and hopfields of her youth to go to the city of dreaming spires as the wife of an Oxford don. Such Gypsy girls may have been acquiescent, but on another occasion, on a windy spring day on which, the singer tells us, 'the old folks were blown far' and 'the young ones were playing', there was a different outcome to one of these Gorjio-Gypsy romancings:

One spring morning a young Squire was straying
Enjoying the beauties that nature provides,
The old folks were blown far, the young ones were playing
And there he beheld such a dark Gypsy lass.
Struck with such beauty, he seemed most delighted
He forgot his descending and familiar pride,
But let her be what she may, either wealthy or lowly,
He swore by the powers he would make her his bride.

'Now here's to your horses, your carriage and splendours
Here's to your horses in green wooded dells,'
Behind the camp-fires two bright eyes were shining
And that's where he first saw his own Gypsy girl.

The unexpected toast to the squire's horses, carriage, and 'splendours' presumably comes from the girl's father who would like to further the match. And the young squire tells her,

'Stay with me now; In a few months I will marry you
The smoke shall be your descending and I shall be your guide,'

He's being extremely tactful. In case she feels she may sometimes be at a loss amid house-dwelling society he explains he'll be there to guide her and the smoke will be her descending in case she feels inadequate about her family tree. Her response, however, is less romantic.

'May I tell your fortune?' 'My dearie, I know it
The fortune I crave for is you for my bride.'

And now for the Gypsy girl's brush-off:

'Do you wish to insult me with all your proposals?
I'm a poor Gypsy girl and you are a Squire,
Through dirt and through mires yet I am light-hearted
Though you ride upon my mead that stands on the green.
I'm a poor Gypsy girl and you are a Squire
With wealth and great beauty it is your command,
But there's more honest hearts in the poor and the lowly
Than all those proud ladies who walk through the land.'

A simple chat up of another proud lady led to a young man being taken off into Elfland, according to the famous traditional song sung by Duncan Williamson. Elfland, she tells him, is 'very far away' and after some conversation he climbs on her horse behind her and rides with her through a countryside whose topographical features become increasingly unusual:

> So they rode and they rode, and merrily merrily rode
> They rode for a night and a day,
> Until they came to a red river
> That lay across their way.
>
> 'What river is this?', O Thomas he said
> 'O please to me do say',
> 'This is a river of blood', she said
> 'That is spilled on a certain one day.'
>
> So they rode and they rode, and merrily merrily rode
> O merrily they rode away,
> Until they came to a crystal river
> That lay across their way.
>
> 'What river is this?', O Thomas he said
> 'O please to me do say',
> 'This is a river of tears', she said
> 'That were spilled on a certain one day.'
>
> O merrily they rode away, and merrily merrily rode
> O merrily they rode away,
> Until they came to a thorny road
> That lay across their way.

'What road is that?', O Thomas he said
'O please to me do tell',
'O that is a road you must never lead
For that road, it leads to hell...'

The folk music of any people survives as a living force by being constantly renewed, new numbers being constantly added to the existing repertoire. Ballads like 'Thomas the Rhymer' and 'Sir Patrick Spens' are printed in anthologies as songs of immense antiquity. Duncan Williamson and other Gypsies are still singing them today, not learned from a book but handed down through who knows how many generations. Through all those centuries Gypsies and other singers have held their audience spellbound as they embarked on the story that tells how:

> *The King sits in Dunfermline town*
> *Drinking the blood-red wine…*

A vivid and detailed memory is an essential for non-literate folk. They are not able to turn to books for information or to keep written records. Gypsies who are not 'scholars' may have a repertoire of hundreds of songs and many Gypsies believe that their non-literacy has been a positive help in building up a successful business. George Smith's parents made many moves, some as part of their search for work, some as the consequence of eviction. Because of these many moves George attended a number of different schools over a number of years:

To me it's never made no sense because I went to four or five different schools in twelve years and my teachers, the way I think of it, they was teaching their own Gorjio pupils and they never paid no attention to me, I mean, I was a newcomer and they didn't ask me what I knowed or if I could read or write or anything, they was just going on teaching their pupils as if I wasn't there. I mean, I went to school for a long long time and I never gained a thing by going to school because they never said to me 'Can you read?' or 'Can you write?' Which I can't read now, or write, not from school learning.

But I'm proud to say that I've come along fine in my life and I can't thank a book and pencil for it. My father couldn't write nor read, my mother couldn't write nor read. But they brung eighteen kids up, I mean, I'm one of them, I'm the Babby of 'em, and I mean I can't say that they never did a bad job in raising me, I mean, I ain't short, I'm married, I've got two kids and they'm following in my footsteps and they'll be all right later on if they go on as they're going on, but I never thanked a pencil or a book for bringing me where I am today.

Mik Darling's 'My Pony and Me' was possibly influenced by Duncan Williamson's 'My Old Horse and Me'. He says of it,

There was a man called Bill Hook who used to run a small scrapyard in the town of Ingleton and he would, if you went down with your pony and cart and gathered up all the old rubbish and stuff, he'd always buy it off you and give you a shilling for it.

However hard it was for these people, it never stopped them singing about it around the fire at night, it's not a miserable song and yet it's a nasty position to be in.

It was snowing hard and blowing so cold
The roughest day that I've ever had,
My legs they were stiff and my fingers froze
Ice was growing on my ears and my nose.

I had no money to feed the kids
So out on the cart I go,
Well, I call at a few farms and some houses as well
Up to the door, and my tale I tell.

'Have you any scrap iron, or furniture or junk?
It's not to buy beer with, I never get drunk,
I'm trying to earn an honest living, you see,
Out in all weathers, my pony and me.

A sadder incident is recalled in 'One Time by Stratford', sung by Tom Odley:

We'd atched up one time, side a place close to Stratford;
Near the village of Sambourne, on a road called Wyke Lane.
The day that we pulled there was right dark and gloomy:
The black clouds above us were pouring down rain.

Now the life of a Traveller is oft far from easy;
For our moments of pleasure, with hardships, we pay!
If some they should tell you, 'It's peaches and honey!'
Then they've never known life the hard Neadi way.

The morning that followed was warm bright and sunny;
This West Midland air seemed so fresh sweet and clear;
But the gavvers arrived at the end of that morning,
To tell us; 'Move on! You mustn't camp here!'

So I says to them; 'Sirs! Why soon we'll be leavin';
For fruitin' will start in but a few days!'
The mush dressed in blue, said, 'See that you do so!
We don't want you here with your wild Gyppo ways!'

That next Friday evening, we sat by the fire;
All happy a-talking of Travellers we'd known;
When the peace of the evening, so rudely, was shattered,
Along with our window, by a brick that was thrown!

Yes; the life of the Traveller is oft far from easy;
For our moments of pleasure, with hardship, we pay;
If some they should tell you, 'It's peaches and honey!'
Then they've never known life the hard Neadi way!

Neadi is, of course, another name for a Gypsy—although not usually one of the purest lineage. In his poem 'Shadows Round the Fire', Tom Odley speaks of the Gypsy race as a whole:

> *...Here today and there awhile*
> *In moments gone in phantom style*
> *Oppressed yet ever free.*
> *In ancient times by city wall*
> *In modern age mid urban sprawl*
> *Their burning fires are seen.*
> *Hungarian hutments, Spanish cave*
> *On English heath, rural enclave*
> *Their shadows, but a while;*
> *Society scorns, the settled folk repel*
> *Alleging that we stem from hell*
> *Our shadows formed by flame.*
> *If truth were told, they are aware*
> *That Gypsies simply do not share*
> *The love of mammon's way.*

Prejudice often runs high against Gypsies and at least one Birmingham Councillor has called for extermination as a solution to the 'Gypsy problem'.

For reasons best perhaps kept to themselves, councils often prefer to use taxpayers' money to harass Gypsy children, women and men, and drive them out of their area, rather than provide sites for them as they were until recently required to do by law.

Over the last twenty-five years, West Midlands Highways Departments have been laying deep ditches across the greensward at the side of our highways traditionally camped on by Gypsies. Often ditching was not enough. Thousands of tons of rock and stone have been dumped to make the Gypsies' traditional parking places unusable.

Local authorities have built many sites but even now there are sites for little more than half of all our Gypsy Travellers.

The Children Act says councils must provide basic amenities such as toilets and running water, for children in need. Few of our roadside Gypsies have that. Not so long ago, judgement was entered in the High Court against the county of Hereford and Worcester for its failure to provide sites and Mr Justice Henry said, 'If there are not sufficient sites where Gypsies may lawfully stop, they will be without the law whenever and wherever they do stop. If moved on, they and their children will suffer from society's failure to provide for them. Their plight will, or should be, an affront to the national conscience.'

At an eviction at Brownhills in Walsall, three little girls, all sisters, and cousins of Johnny 'Pops' Connors, were burned to death when a Calor gas stove turned over and set fire to the caravan in which they were sleeping, as it was towed away. The parents had not been there to put out the stove before the caravan was moved because they had been taken away by police officers for questioning. Before singing the ballad in which he describes this, Johnny Connors says:

For a solid week we were shifted from night, noon and day, night, noon and day, handed over from police to police.

Brownhills, Staffordshire. The Travellers were evicted from the site by the Brownhills Urban District Council, assisted by the Birmingham Corporation, and by the police, in fact by 100 police. That's when the battle started.

The next morning I went and I found 27 Travellers and I brought them all to Copperside and for 17 days the battle went on.

In the second eviction in Walsall, in George Street car park, three little sisters, three cousins of mine, was burned to death when the police tore [the parents] out of the caravan. What else can I say? Me song, I think, will tell the story.

In a voice almost inarticulate with grief, Johnny Connors sings how:

> *...When the squad cars of those licensed thugs*
> *Came to tow our trailers away*
> *Three children, three little girls*
> *Asleep in bed they lay.*
> *May the Lord have mercy on their souls,*
> *They died in that eviction that day.*
>
> *At the graveyard at Bilston*
> *We laid them in their grave.*
> *Our hearts were filled with sorrow,*
> *Our heads were filled with shame,*
> *It is the wicked and cruel law of the land*
> *That we have to blame.*
> *And please God, in all good time,*
> *The human-minded people'll find...*
> *The travellers a place to stay!*

Like 'The Poor Old Man', this song is also about a tragedy that overcame the Connors. Like 'The Poor Old Man', this lament too will doubtless pass into the Gypsy repertoire, and future singers will one day be wondering what were the tragic circumstances of the event it describes. That tombstone in Bilston graveyard will provide a tragic footnote.

'You treat us like dirt,' sings Paddy Houlahan, 'with no feelings to get hurt.' It is particularly distressing to Gypsies with their high standards of hygiene that they are frequently denied running water and refuse collection. It is not surprising that their outside environment looks sometimes rather like the streets of London did at the time that the refuse collectors went on strike. In the circumstances it is remarkable how spotlessly turned out our Gypsies are, and how immaculate the insides of their caravans. 'Is it us? Or the Gorjio people?' asks a song sung by Ezekiel Warner:

> *They say we leave litter and mess up the land*
> *We're the dirty Gypsy people,*
> *But who laid the blight on each meadow and strand?*
> *Was it us? Or the Gorjio people?*
>
> *They say we're a menace to the health of the land*
> *The unhealthy travelling people,*
> *But who poisons the air and rivers everywhere?*
> *Is it us? Or the Gorjio people?*
>
> *They say we're dishonest, no better than rogues*
> *The thieving travelling people,*
> *But who kills for gain, robs banks and holds up trains?*
> *Is it us? Or the Gorjio people?*
>
> *They say we're quarrelsome, given to blows*
> *The violent travelling people,*
> *But who starts the wars, breaks the first of human laws?*
> *Is is us? Or the Gorjio people?*

They say we are backward, retarded and slow
The ignorant travelling people,
But who judges and condemns for his own ends?
Why you do! The Gorjio people.

Occasionally songs are to be heard in full Romani rather than
the Anglo-Romani used these days by British Gypsies:

Opré Roma

Gelem, gelem, lungone dromensa.
Maladilem bahtale Romesa.

A Romale, A Cavale.

A Romale katar tumen aven,
E tsarensa bahtale dromensa?

A Romale, A Cavale.

Vi man sas bari familija,
Mudardas la e kali legija.

A Romale, A Cavale.

Aven mansa sa lumniake Roma,
Kai putaile e romane droma.

A Romale, A Cavale.

66

Ake vriama, usti Rom akana,
Men hutasa misto kai kerasa!

A Romale, A Cavale.

The richness of the Gypsy culture has been largely ignored by non-Gypsies just as has their huge contribution to the prosperity of agricultural areas like the West Midlands. Those days when they dealt in hundreds of horses and were always there just in time to save the harvest, and were born in bender tents because it was believed it made them stronger, are still very real to Gypsies.

These are dark days. The anti-Gypsy legislation of 1994 was not unlike that of Germany in the early thirties and we, Gypsies included, know where that led. Our West Midland counties have dragged their feet in finding sites so that hundreds of families still have nowhere legal to site their caravans.

With Bill Kerswell, vice president of the National Gypsy Council, I visit a fine Gypsy singer. She is magnificent. She has recently been moved from her caravan and housed in a flat. She is afraid to sing to us because, she says, the neighbours don't like it. Yet the blare of the neighbours' television is clearly audible.

It is to the European Community that our Gypsies can begin to look in hope. Though deprivation and humiliation of Gypsies goes on there, as here, the million Gypsies of the Community have been given the status of an officially recognised racial group and millions of pounds are now available for Gypsies to claim their rights in education, civil rights, and to somewhere where they can legally be.

'Opré Roma', adapted from a lament originally sung by Gypsies in the German extermination camps, has been adopted as their anthem. To the three tragic original verses of the lament have been added two more, adding a message of hope.

Roughly translated, 'Opré Roma' goes:

Rise Up, Gypsies …

Once I travelled on the long roads,
Everywhere meeting happy Gypsies.

O Gypsy men, O young men of the Gypsies.

O Gypsies, who can tell where you come from,
With your tents beside the joyful roads?

O Gypsy men, O young men of the Gypsies.

Once I had a mighty family,
But the Black Legion took them all away.

O Gypsy men, O young men of the Gypsies.

But come with me now, Gypsies from all the world,
For the Gypsy roads are once again beginning to open for us.

O Gypsy men, O young men of the Gypsies.

Now is the time, let us rise up Gypsies now,
Now we will go far if only we unite in action.

O Gypsy men, O young men of the Gypsies.

69

Cold Blows the Wind (The Unquiet Grave) sung by Alfred Price Jones (1912)

On Christmas Day it Happened So sung by Esther Smith (c.1910)

Under the Leaves; or The Seven Virgins sung by Angelina Whatton (c.1910)

Christ Made A Trance sung by Angelina Whatton (c.1910)

As It Fell Out on My 'Oliday sung by Gypsies at Sutton St Nicholas (c.1910)

There is a Fountain of Christs Blood sung by Esther & Eliza Smith (c.1910)

71

For a Blacksmith He Courted Me (The Blacksmith) sung by Harriett Jones (c.1910)

My Father Rises Early (Standing Round the Campfire) composed & sung by Paddy Houlahan (1994) ©

The Books you read at school (Crossing Their Line) words by Paddy Houlahan © (1994)
Music by W. Graham ©

Last bar once more for second verse

72

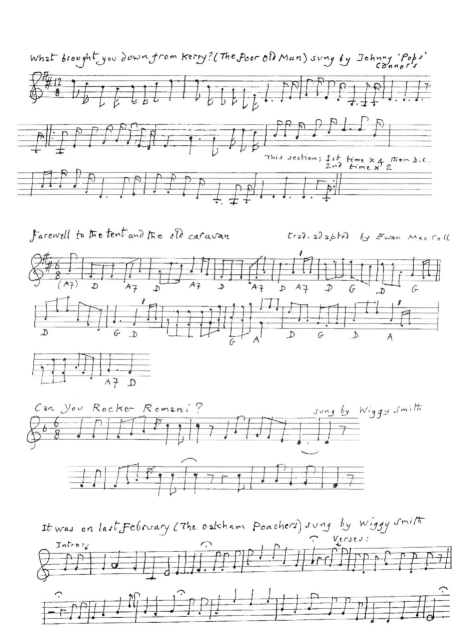

What brought you down from Kerry? (The Poor Old Man) sung by Johnny 'Pops' Connors

This section; 1st time X 4 then D.C.
2nd time x 2

Farewell to the tent and the old caravan   trad. adapted by Ewan MacColl

Can You Rocker Romani?   sung by Wiggy Smith

It was on last February (The oakham Poachers) sung by Wiggy Smith

Intro: Verses:

74

The Rich Farmer from Sheffield   sung by Wiggy Smith

I was once young and foolish (The Deserter)   sung by Wiggy Smith
1st verse

2nd & 3rd verse

Old Lankin   sung by Tony Lloyd

← This is the basic tune but there is also a variation for the maid when she saw her master.

etc

.The Raggle Taggle Gypsies and Lord Cassilis   sung by Mik and Susie Darling
(A) Dm A Dm A Dm A Dm A DmGmD C F   Am Dm F   C
Dm A   Dm

Mandi went to Pooye the Grai   sung by Amos Smith

75

The Little Gypsy Girl — sung by Lil Loveridge

The Squire and the Gypsy — sung by Lil Loveridge

Thomas the Rhymer — sung by Duncan Williamson

Is it Us? Or the Gorjio People? — sung by Ezekiel Warner

Tail piece

INDEX OF SONG TITLES AND FIRST LINES